Dreams: God's Voice in the Night

Interpret Your Own Dreams with Ease and Accuracy

By
Barbara Lardinais

DESTINY IMAGE® PUBLISHERS, INC.

P.O. Box 310, Shippensburg, PA 17257-0310

"*Promoting Inspired Lives.*"

This book and all other Destiny Image and Destiny Image Fiction books are available at Christian bookstores and distributors worldwide.

Cover design by: Eileen Rockwell

For more information on foreign distributors, call 717-532-3040.

Or reach us on the Internet: www.destinyimage.com

ISBN 13 TP: 978-0-7684-0746-4

ISBN 13 EBook: 978-0-7684-0747-1

For Worldwide Distribution, Printed in the U.S.A.

1 2 3 4 5 6 /17 16 15 14

DEDICATION

For my mother, Mary Lucille, who is now with the Lord. Thanks, Mom, for passing on a family heritage so rich in Irish dreamers.

ACKNOWLEDGMENTS

A heart of thanksgiving for Jessica and Danielle, not only my daughters, but my two best friends. Your prayers and encouragement carried me through this process.

Special thanks to Jenni Miller who gave me invaluable technical advice and assistance.

CONTENTS

INTRODUCTION

Dreams are one of the most fascinating topics in all the earth. I know by the vast volumes of mail I receive about dreams. After over thirty years of personal study and dream-interpretation experience, I added a section about dreams to my website, www.hannahscupboard.com. It seemed to me there was a great need for Christians to have a resource to understand how God was speaking through their dreams. Since that section exploded in popularity almost immediately, I guess I really hit the mark.

What does it mean when I dream about bears?

Last night I dreamed about my mother who has been gone for ten years...

I've had this recurring dream for the past three years...

I've been fascinated with dreams since I was a small child and my family would share their dreams around the breakfast table. My mother was a prophetic dreamer, and when I hadn't seen her for a while I'd ask, *"Had any dreams lately, Mom?"*

We *all* dream even though some will say they don't. Most of us remember at least shadows of some of our dreams. Some dreams are puzzling and some are scary and some seem more real than awake life. Moreover, we sense that some dreams are messages from God; and if that is the case, we want to understand exactly what He is saying to us.

The dream language is quite different from any other language we may have mastered. It's more visual than verbal, filled with symbols and images rather than words. We need some kind of Dream School to get a handle on how to translate our dreams accurately into our own native tongue.

This book is Dream School 101 for those who would like to know how to interpret their own dreams. Getting down some basic principles will take away a lot of the mystery and open up a whole new world for understanding dreams and determining their source.

As I started writing this book, the song "Dream a Little Dream of Me" kept going through my head. The first stanza goes:

> *Stars shining bright above you,*
> *Night breezes seem to whisper, "I love you."*
> *Birds singin' in the sycamore trees,*
> *"Dream a little dream of me."*
> (1931, lyrics by Gus Kahn)

In my view for this book, God is the singer, calling us to the most wonderful sleep. His Word promises, *"When you lie down, you will not be afraid; when you lie down, your sleep will be sweet*" (Proverbs 3:24). By connecting to Him in our dream world, this will always be true. May it be true for *every* one of your dreams.

CHAPTER 1

Determining the Source of Your Dream

The year was 1969 and our country was in the throes of the tumultuous war in Vietnam. Protests were raging everywhere, including the campus of New York University at Stony Brook where my husband attended graduate school. Even though the war hung over us each day like a dark shadow, I quietly began to breathe some tentative sighs of relief. Surely it was unlikely at this point that he would be drafted. Not impossible, but maybe we were out of the woods. Whew!

One night I had a very clear dream where the war was center stage and the emotions attached to it were very strong. In fact, the power of the dream remains with me after more than forty years. It was a prophetic dream, but I had no idea of that at the time. I was not yet a Christian and I had no sense of what God was speaking to me, but speaking to me He was. The dream went like this.

My husband, David, had been drafted and sent to the fierce front line in Vietnam. He was in a foxhole and, unbelievably, I was in there with him—just the two of us. I was on his right side and I had a job if I was willing to stay. In actual fact, David had almost no hearing in his right ear, probably from a childhood illness. Being deaf in a war zone could certainly be deadly, so in the dream I was allowed to stay with him and be his right ear. I had a clear understanding within the dream that I was free to go at any time, my choice.

I cannot express how desperately I wanted to get out of there. The full horror of the war was upon me. Bombs exploded continuously and I made David aware of each approaching danger. Dread choked me. But as badly as I wanted out, I was still more terrified that if I left the battle my husband might be killed. I just couldn't do it. So I stayed, even if reluctantly.

It ended like that. I'm pretty sure it woke me up. So vivid and horrible, the dream made me feel afterward that I really understood what it was like being in real battle. This was no ordinary dream and I speculated on what it might mean. Was David going to be drafted after all? But no, Vietnam came nowhere near us and our life went on. I never forgot it, but eventually it receded to my closet of mysteries. It would be nearly nine years before I had some inkling of what God was saying.

Dreaming may seem to be one of the more exotic ways to hear from God. At least we in the Western world feel that way; the other half of the world takes it for granted, and in biblical times it was assumed that God spoke through dreams as a natural part of life. The Bible is chock-full of dreams that meant something—not just the standard run of the mill dreams most of us have routinely.

- It was during a dream that God revealed to Abraham the history of the descendants he would have and the 400-year Egyptian captivity (Genesis 15).

- Jacob had a dream, as he lay on the ground with a stone for a pillow, in which he saw a ladder ascending to heaven with angels going up and down (Genesis 28).

- Joseph dreamed he would someday rule over all his brothers and even his father (Genesis 37). Later, in chapter 41, Joseph correctly interprets the Pharaoh's dream.

- Daniel understood the interpretation of dreams and was able to escape death by explaining to Nebuchadnezzar the dream he had and the unfolding of the king's future (Daniel 2).

- In the New Testament, Joseph was told to accept Mary as his wife because the child she was having was conceived by the Holy Spirit (Matthew 1).

- The wise men from the East were divinely warned in a dream to return to their own country by a different route and not return to tell Herod the location of the baby Jesus (Matthew 2).

- Pilate's wife sent word to her husband not to have anything to do with Jesus because she *"suffered many things today in a dream because of Him"* (Matthew 27:19 NKJV).

Dreams abound in the Bible, and we can assume that as God spoke to people then, He is still speaking to us in the same way today. But even though dreams from God are flourishing today, not *every* dream is of divine origin. Spiritually speaking, dreams can come from three sources: divine origin, demonic origin, or soulish (our own mind and emotions) origin. Dreams of divine origin come from the Holy Spirit and are sometimes called prophetic dreams. How can you tell when a dream is prophetic or from God?

To many people, the word *prophetic* has to do with foretelling future events, but that is only one shade of its meaning in God's Word. Prophecy, more simply put, is any utterance from God. A prophetic dream is one in which God is speaking something and it may not necessarily regard a future event. For instance, a prophetic dream can bring confirmation, comfort, warning, or direction.

Divine Origin

Two types of dreams serve to cue us that the source may be directly from God: *recurring dreams* and ones I call *uniquely vibrant dreams.* This does not mean that God is not speaking through non-recurring dreams or the common ordinary ones. It also does not mean that every reoccurring dream is prophetic—but I will say that the uniquely vibrant ones nearly always are.

Recurring Dreams

If you have the same dream or a slightly varying dream over and over for months or even years, pay attention to that. I learned early on to pay very close attention to my mother when she said she had a dream more than once. I never saw one instance where it turned out that God was not speaking through the dream in some way. A track record is a good barometer for confirmation even though you may have to wait a few years to establish it. This makes it a good reason to begin to notice and keep track of your dreams.

A reoccurring dream may signal a warning from God about a life event, or it may work to show dreamers the state of something in their lives. For instance, my mother dreamed for two full years that one of her children would be separated from her child for an extended period of time. This event did come to pass. I believe my mother's prayers helped to prepare, soften, and avert greater disaster in this situation.

In my own life, for years I had a recurring dream that centered on taking off in an airplane. Eventually I caught on to the themes in the dream, so I spent much prayer and pondering for its meaning. Over time I came to realize that the dream was revealing part of the state of my life and something very deep that I was working through. Finally the dream changed substantially; and with deep relief, I knew the issue had been worked to completion.

Unique, Vibrant Dreams

The only way to describe it is to say that this kind of dream is just plain different. It has a different feel from the regular nightly run of dreams that you are used to. I have probably had less than ten of these in my lifetime. It is a dream kicked up about ten notches. They are clear, rich, vibrant, unusual, and very memorable. This is not the dream that you have to catch first thing in the morning before it quickly recedes and is out of reach. This is a dream you can't forget. It may feel so important that it wakes you up. I'm not including nightmares in this explanation. They also may be quite startling and memorable, but in a bad way. I will discuss nightmares more fully in the next section.

Another characteristic is that over time, it is still fresh. This is probably the way Joseph's dream felt when he dreamed of the shafts of wheat bowing down to him in Genesis 37. When he awoke, he knew this was different and he had a pretty good idea that God was speaking. His is also a case where the meaning of the dream did not become entirely clear or fulfilled for many years. Whenever the meaning of a dream is not entirely clear, put it on a shelf and wait. Eventually it will be exposed; and if it is really from God, you will not have forgotten it.

Demonic Origin

It's not that hard to identify dreams with demonic origin. The harder part is to identify any underlying causes contributing to them. Hardest still is to *stop* them and yet that's the thing the dreamer is most interested in. We will talk about this further, but first let's determine how you can tell if your dream is coming from the pit of hell.

Notice some common threads of these dreams sent to me over the years:

From the age of seven I have been having dreams about demons attacking my family. They are violent, sadistic, and seem completely real when I'm dreaming them.

For years I have had dreams that consist of Satan trying to take over me. Most of the time I cannot really see this figure but I feel him and awake before he ever touches me.

I have these debilitating dreams that lock me down by demons. I was once in occult activity and I was also sexually abused as a child. Lately there are hands that grab and poke my body. Some even try to go between my legs.

I have had this dream since I was about seven or eight. I go into a deep sleep and can't wake or scream. I feel or see that something is trying to hurt me and it's often an ugly face that I don't know.

As you can see, most people are perfectly aware when their dream is demonically provoked. In fact, if you have the sense that the dream is demonic, it probably is. Terror, violence, horror, sadism, perversity, abnormality, and a sense of evil characterize these kinds of dreams. Of course that's the complete opposite of God's desire for our sleep. He means it for our daily restoration. Psalm 4:8 tells us, *"In peace I will both lie down and sleep, for You alone, O Lord, make me to dwell in safety."* Demonic dreams produce feelings of hopelessness, futility, paralyzing fear, and panic, to name a few. The person wakes up demoralized and depressed, not refreshed and rested.

Do all nightmares fall under the category of demonic origin? Usually perhaps, but not in every case. First we must consider and eliminate the possibility of physical or natural causes. Certain medical conditions or medications can produce nightmares. While recovering from surgery, I was once given a pain medication that produced nightmares and hallucinations that I still shutter to remember. Additionally we must consider severe trauma. A horrific event in the life of the dreamer can cause nightmares that may not point back to a demonic origin.

Where there are nightmares that cannot be attributed to any physical or natural cause, we must next ask these questions: Why? What opened the door to the subconscious dream world that allowed access? While God may give a strong warning or have dramatic events show up in a dream so He can say something particular to us, we will not feel terrified or unsafe.

The following is part of an email I received from a Christian lady who desperately wanted to understand why she was having nightmares and how to stop them.

> *I have had nightmares as far back as I can remember. I still can recall dreams I had as a child. Some are very scary and others are very perverse. I have been a Christian for 15 years and asked God to set me free from this, but I still have them. I also have a sister who suffers from the same thing.*

When I read about her nightmares, I was initially struck by the fact that her reoccurring dreams had gone on so long—since childhood. That seemed very significant to me. Even more significant is that the dreamer had a sister *"who suffers from the same thing."* I believe that's particularly important and not just a coincidence.

What happened to these two sisters in childhood to trigger nightmares so severe they continued well into adulthood? I can propose a few possibilities. Were they separately or together sexually abused or molested, perhaps when they were too young to comprehend exactly what was happening? Or, did they live in a home with intense violence, especially at night? Third, did any adults ever use them in occult activities such as satanic rituals or ceremonies?

The fact that both sisters had the same kind of dream is a dead giveaway that *something* happened to them when they were children that sparked the nightmares. Getting to that root could solve the "why" of these sisters' nightmares, a necessary step in eliminating them.

The most common root element I've found that causes nightmares, particularly reoccurring nightmares, is occult or satanic activity. Upon questioning, over and over dreamers usually admit that they or their parents have been involved in some type of occult activity. It's like handing Satan a permission slip. Is it any wonder the Lord lovingly warns us:

> *There shall not be found among you anyone who makes his son or his daughter pass through the fire, one who uses divination, one who practices witchcraft, or one who interprets omens, or a sorcerer, or one who casts a spell, or a medium, or a spiritist, or one who calls up the dead (Deuteronomy 18:10-11).*

Sleep should be a time of rest and refreshment. Often it is a time of hearing from God in a special way. *"When you lie down, you will not be afraid; when you lie down, your sleep will be sweet"* (Proverbs 3:24). Sweet sleep. That's what we should expect. None of us is destined for a lifetime of nightmares so we shouldn't put up with them as if they are normal. I suggest an all-out assault on this infringement of your freedom in Christ until victory is secured!

Soulish Realm Origin

In the scientific realm, dreaming has been somewhat mysterious, but now there is tremendous research going on to better understand why we dream and how often. Even people who claim not to remember dreams do dream. Tests on sleep deprivation prove that sleep and the accompaniment of dreams is a necessity we cannot live without.

Probably 99 percent of all dreams come from a mix of our own mind and emotions—the soulish realm, with the influence of the current events of our lives. These are the bread and butter of our dream world: illogical fragments, juxtapositions, time out of sequence, incoherent events, and bits of this and that come crowding one into the next during our nighttime slumber.

So, just because they originate out of our souls, does it mean they aren't from God? No. Dreaming is part of God's design for our health and well-being. I remember going through a very stressful computer conversion once in which several solutions to problems came to me in dreams. I would wake up in the middle of the night and write down what I got through dreaming and implement it the next day at work. I also previously mentioned my long-term dreams about taking off in an airplane. They weren't prophetic dreams, but they were from God anyhow in the sense that they enabled me to process parts of my life that made me more whole as a person.

Appreciate your nightly journey into the deepest reaches of your mind whether you remember much of the dreams or not and even if some of them make little sense. As you begin to try to understand your own dreams, it's important to remember that just like your heart or your lungs have a purpose for your body, dreams have a purpose, too. Dreaming can be a connection to areas deep within yourself being worked through in ways you cannot manage in your awake state.

Some of the dream symbols we will talk about will help with this type of dream just as much as with those important prophetic dreams.

CHAPTER 2

Dream Types and God's Purposes

Warning Dreams

God uses dreams to speak to us about all the issues of life. One of the most dramatic is the warning dream. There is an interesting example in Genesis 20. Abraham and Sarah journeyed to a place called Gerar where a king named Abimelech ruled. Out of fear, Abraham presented Sarah as his sister rather than his wife. This was a half-truth as Sarah was actually his half-sister. The king sent for Sarah to be his wife as she was exceedingly beautiful; but before he had any relations with her, he had a dream.

God got his attention fast by saying to him straight out, *"Indeed you are a dead man because of the woman whom you have taken, for she is a man's wife"* (Genesis 20:3 NKJV). The king argued with God within the dream that he had not done this intentionally; God agreed and told him to return

Sarah and have Abraham pray for him, otherwise he was going to die. Sarah was returned and the king lived.

While some dreams need interpretation and are filled with symbols, the warning dream is usually more straightforward. This was also the case in the dream Joseph had after the baby Jesus was born. An angel was sent by God in the dream to say, *"Arise, take the young Child and His mother, flee to Egypt, and stay there until I bring you word; for Herod will seek the young Child to destroy Him"* (Matthew 2:13 NKJV).

Why is a warning dream sent? Usually God is giving us advance information so that something *can be averted*. The important part to remember is that some action on our part can turn the tide. For Joseph, that action was to arise immediately and obey God's command to flee the country to protect the Child. Often, the action we need to take is to pray.

I once had a warning dream that I unfortunately did not discern well enough to avert what was ahead. On a bright, sunny Saturday morning in January many years ago, my home was burglarized. I had left the house about midday to do some errands, and when I returned after about two hours, my home had been broken into and robbed of all small electronic devices and every bit of jewelry. According to the police, everything that could be taken quickly was carried away easily on foot.

If you have suffered a similar incident, you know it carries a strong sense of personal violation. Additionally for me, I was thinking about the spiritual perspective. Where was God in this? What happened? In my case, I almost immediately remembered a dream I had had just three months to the day prior to the burglary. I had been warned of this impending event, and now I could see that clearly. Even at the time I knew that the dream was significant, and that's an important point in interpreting dreams.

Here's the dream:

> *I was in a park on a lovely day. I casually crossed a walkway from a park bench where I had been sitting. Suddenly realizing I had left my purse on the bench, I looked back to see that it was gone. It had been stolen and I knew that it was my own fault, careless negligence. Without my purse, all the information that I needed to help myself was missing. I felt an overwhelming sense of guilt and stupidity. I mentally kicked myself over and over because of a mess that had been so avoidable. "If only..." played repeatedly in my brain.*

When I awoke, the dream was near and very vivid and the feelings associated with it were extremely strong. The strength of emotions is a clue that a dream may be out of the ordinary. Normal dreams usually fade fast. So pay attention to strong emotion.

Feeling sure that my dream represented a warning of some type, I began to analyze vulnerabilities regarding the contents of my purse in particular. Did I have a file with copies of important documents like my driver's license and credit cards? Did I have the right phone numbers to call in case of theft? Was I being careful enough in restaurants or while shopping? Should I tighten up the overall security of my household?

One of the areas that definitely needed tightening was my general carelessness in locking doors. I had grown complacent during a time when I owned a large, protective German Shepherd. Really, with him around, there was no need for locks, but he had been gone several years. I had never completely reverted to consistent locking. So I started to lock doors again—but not every single time.

You guessed it; my doors weren't locked the day of the burglary. I gave way to laziness since it was broad daylight and I wasn't going to be gone long. After all, I lived in such a safe neighborhood where everyone watched out for each other. Plus, it had been three whole months since the dream and nothing had come about.

When I returned home and realized what had happened, I felt exactly like I had in the dream. Like it was entirely my fault—completely avoidable. I really blew it, right? What good was the warning since I never heeded it? Not true. Having had the dream did help me in some important ways. After I had it, I had begun saying special prayers for protection of my possessions and myself. You may think I was unsuccessful there, too, but again, not true. As I look back at what happened and what was taken (and what was not taken), I see how God contained the incident. He allowed so much, but no more.

I wish it had not happened, but it did permanently knock out of me my lackadaisical indifference to security. As strong as the dream was, it had obviously not changed my daily living patterns. Eventually I realized that the dream got my attention—but the burglary changed my behavior. Perhaps that was God's ultimate protection for me in the end. Perhaps the two things together worked to restrain a far worse incident that will never happen and that I won't know about till eternity. Regardless, my dream will always remain a source of comfort to me.

Prayer over warning dreams can change an outcome or diminish an adverse impact. I believe this was definitely true in my case. If you have such a dream, know that the dream does not indicate that things are set in stone. Usually that is not the case. God tells us things, especially future things, for a reason. Prayer is partnering with God for His purposes to be fulfilled in the earth.

Don't take a fatalist attitude regarding any warning dreams you may have. Actually, the dream is a sign of hope. God may be informing you that *without* prayer, this is going to happen. Therefore, **pray.** *"The prayer of a* *righteous person is powerful and effective"* (James 5:16b New International Version).

Revelation Dreams

What if you had just cheated someone out of their rightful inheritance and now you are on the run from their justifiable wrath? What would you think of the likelihood of God giving you a wonderful dream confirming His future plans for great good in your life? Well, that's exactly what happened to Jacob, a cheat and a manipulator. Remember that God always sees us for what He can make of us, not the worst of what we are now.

Jacob's dream happened as he lay alone on a stone pillow out in the wilderness. He saw a ladder ascending from the earth to the heavens, and God spoke the same promise He had made to his grandfather, Abraham: *"Your descendants will also be like the dust of the earth, and you will spread out to the west and to the east and to the north and to the south; and in you and in your descendants shall all the families of the earth be blessed"* (Genesis 28:14).

Beyond the promise, He also comforted Jacob: *"Behold, I am with you and will keep you wherever you go, and will bring you back to this land; for I will not leave you until I have done what I have promised you"* (v. 15). Considering all that would transpire over Jacob's lifetime, these words were merciful of God indeed.

In this particular dream, God spoke plainly and there was no need to interpret symbols. Perhaps you will also have such a dream, but I will say that it is unusual. Often there are symbols that need to be understood. A friend of mine once had such a dream. In it, a prominent ministry leader appeared with a terribly disfiguring, almost mortal wound to the head. He was shriveled and emaciated and being carried by others through a large crowd, and he couldn't speak.

When my friend awoke, she knew something was very wrong in the ministry leader's life. She had a sense that it was not an actual physical wound but something moral that was affecting his ability to minister effectively. This dream proved an accurate picture. Within a year of the dream, an ugly scandal about him erupted publicly. Many stood by him or "carried" him. The truth about the events was never fully known, and he always denied the accusations. His ministry, however, just barely survived, and his sphere of influence diminished greatly.

The revelation dream is one that may confirm something (like Jacob's dream confirmed his divine destiny) or reveal the state of affairs of something. "Well," you might ask, "if I have such a dream, what do I do with it?" That depends. It can be tricky to decide what action if any is called for, so you will definitely need divine wisdom. Thankfully, God is amply supplied with it and very willing to share it with us: *"But if any of you lacks wisdom, let him ask of God, who gives to all men generously and without reproach, and it will be given to him"* (James 1:5).

Be careful about sharing revelation dreams. If the dream is for you, then you may want to keep it to yourself rather than open it up to random opinions of others. If the dream is about someone else, particularly like my friend's dream about the minister, use extreme caution. You do not want to initiate gossip or speculation, and you may not understand the dream's true meaning. In the case of my friend, she knew that her role was simply to pray. God trusted her with the dream, and she was trustworthy to properly handle it.

Encouragement Dreams

Sometimes all we need to move forward is a little push of encouragement and then God comes along and supplies it with a special dream. Gideon, in the Old Testament, was just a regular guy, a simple farmer who had no natural boldness, and yet God called him to defeat Israel's enemy, Midian. He was the most unlikely of candidates, and I can't say I blame him for his hesitation.

It was a dream Gideon overheard that gave him the courage he needed. God told him to go down to the enemy's camp at night and take his servant Purah with him. While they were there, he listened to one man relate a dream to his friend, and his friend immediately interpreted it. Surprisingly, the friend correctly interpreted what was going to happen through Gideon: *"This is nothing less than the sword of Gideon the son of Joash, a man of Israel; God has given Midian and all the camp into his hand"* (Judges 7:14).

How ironic that God used the dream of the enemy to embolden the man he had chosen to defeat them. At any rate, doubt and hesitation were replaced by resolve. Gideon went back to the camp of Israel and said to his little band of 300, *"Arise, for the Lord has given the camp of Midian into your hands"* (Judges 7:15).

One of the most encouraging dreams I have ever had didn't embolden me to do anything, but it did confirm me in the particular place God called me to at the time. I was getting up about 5 o'clock every morning and joining a small band of intercessors at my church to pray for an hour for all the needs of the church. Then I would speed home to shower and breakfast and get ready for a full workday. My church was about a half-hour drive from my house, so I used the travel time to pray for more personal and family needs.

The effort and motivation needed to keep this up were challenging over time. I thought of skipping or giving up, but somehow I kept on going. One month turned into the next and finally a couple of years went by. Somewhere along the way I had this wonderful dream:

> *I dreamed I was working in my own garden just before dawn. I sensed that I always worked there in the very early morning while it was still dark. As I tended my flowerbeds and dug out weeds, gradually blackness started to give way to gray. It crossed my mind that I wondered why I didn't feel*

unsafe being out in the dark alone. Rather, there was a lovely feeling of being alone but not lonely. But the strongest emotion I felt was satisfaction. I was so deeply satisfied in my gardening that even as I think back on my dream, the feeling overtakes me and it's been more than twenty years.

Can you easily interpret my dream? You might think that's surely a no-brainer, but I didn't relate it to my daily prayer time for quite a while. Being an avid gardener, I thought it was a dream of my soul, simply playing out the joys of something I loved to do. Still, the strength of my emotions and the fact that the dream stayed with me told me there was more to it.

I don't know how long it took, but finally the Holy Spirit switched on the light. The garden was the garden of prayer and I was cultivating things that would bear much fruit. There is deep satisfaction in that. The deepest satisfaction came from knowing that God approved my daily trek to the church, and He was encouraging me. Once I understood that, I was strengthened to continue.

Dreams that Reveal the Future

If God reveals the future to you in a dream, receive it with deep humility, never arrogance. Joseph was only seventeen years of age when the Lord showed him in two dreams that he would ultimately rule over all his brothers and even his father. Oh dear young Joseph, maybe you should have kept those dreams to yourself. But then, of course, the actual telling of the dreams to his family played into their fulfillment, so who knows?

It was jealousy that caused Joseph's brothers to sell him into Egyptian slavery and tell their father Jacob that he had been killed by a wild beast. The whole story is told in Genesis chapters 37 through 50, and it has quite a few dramatic twists and turns so it's worth the full read.

I wonder what Joseph thought through the years about those dreams. After all, he was falsely accused of trying to seduce his master's wife and then languished in a prison cell on foreign soil for years. Did he hold fast to the dream's fulfillment even though it seemed beyond possibility? Did he feel that his foolishness in sharing the dreams altered the outcome? Did he just forget about the dreams as unsolved mysteries?

Whatever he thought, since the dreams were actually from God, they did come to pass in God's timing. That's what we need to keep in mind regarding any such dreams we may have. If they are truly from God, they will come to pass. Most of the time, they can simply be put on a shelf because it is usually only in the fulfillment that real understanding comes.

I have friends who tend to dream of future events, but it is uncommon for me. Still, I did have a dream in which a particular detail revealed a little piece of the future to me, but there was no way for me to understand it until afterward.

I was sitting on an old-fashioned yellow school bus with my ex-husband, David, and it was night. The bus was traveling and we were the only ones on it; I was not even aware of a driver. Although there was more to the dream, the important detail for this illustration is that David was sitting in the first row and I was sitting in the second. When I awoke I had no doubt the dream was from God. The emotions of the dream were very strong. But why was David sitting in the first row while I was in the second?

I puzzled and puzzled over this for several years, but when he died in 2011, I finally understood at least that portion of the dream. The school bus was the school of life and we traveled some of it together. He was sitting in the row ahead of me because he was going to die first. There is no way I could have interpreted it beforehand—and I'm glad I couldn't. Still, that detail had bothered me, and it is a good idea to pay closer attention to any details of a dream that bothers you.

Why does God sometimes reveal the future? I can speculate and perhaps come up with various valid reasons but, in the end, I don't really know. Why does God give us information sometimes but not other times? In the case of my dream about David and the school bus, though, all I can say is that the detail I spoke of has given me a sense of the solidness of God and His purposes. He is never taken by surprise, and He has ordered my steps as well as David's.

Dreams that Instruct

I like this kind of dream because it eliminates confusion for sure. When an angel appeared to Joseph in a
dream and told him not to be afraid to take Mary as his
wife because *"the Child who has been conceived in her is of the
Holy Spirit"* (Matthew 1:20), it must have been an enormous
relief. Guesswork gone. This would be the first of several
instruction dreams God gave the earthly father of Jesus.
Joseph must have been a wise, mature man, because he had
enough sense to obey his dreams rather than question or
ignore them.

If you are certain your dream is from God, be sure to be
like Joseph and obey the instructions. I had an instructional
dream once that had a very "unsavory" aspect to it and yet,
as you will see, it worked well to instruct me. I had been
going to my church for almost seventeen years and, in fact,
this was the same church where I had attended the early
morning intercession I spoke about earlier. As far as I was
concerned, I would be there for the rest of my life.

God had other plans. When one pastor left and another
one came, things changed dramatically. Unhappily, there
was a new direction and divisions began to simmer. My
view was that we would intercede harder; and even though
people began to leave, I intended to stay and see things
through.

One night I had this dream:

The whole congregation was at church to have a meal. People picked up their plate in the fellowship hall but then took it in the sanctuary and ate there. I thought, why are we eating in the sanctuary instead of at the tables in the fellowship hall? The other thing was what we were eating. A big scoop of smelly, wet, canned dog food was put on each person's plate. I can still remember how nauseating it smelled.

I said to a friend, "I just can't do this, I can't eat dog food." She always put a positive spin on everything and replied, "Just pour this pancake syrup over it." I noticed that was what other people were doing, so I got the syrup and headed into the sanctuary; but no matter how hard I tried, I couldn't take a bite. Then I woke up.

It didn't take much to interpret the dream. I got it almost instantaneously. We were being served the spiritual equivalent of dog food from the pulpit. No amount of syrup was going to mask it. A church is a place for spiritual nourishment and this was now a place where the meals were certainly unsavory. I knew the dream was not only my permission to leave the church—it was also my command. How much longer would I have held on if not for the dream?

Instruction dreams are a call for action of some type. Start doing something. Stop doing something. Move.

Change direction. They may be obvious, or the dreams may have symbols you will need to interpret. If there are symbols and they aren't as clear as my "dog food dream," pray before you proceed until you are sure of what to do next.

Have I covered all the dream types relating to the purposes of God here? *No.* God may have many other intentions for dreams, but this sampling does cover some of the most common types of dreams. Sometimes when we understand our dream, we then understand why God gave it to us. With some dreams, we have to wait a long time to gain that understanding. My Vietnam dream was one like that, but as you will see, God's timing is always perfect.

CHAPTER 3

Common Sense Guidelines to
Dream Interpretation

How had we gotten to this place, so far from where we started? When I married my husband, David, I was convinced I knew the end of the story: "and they lived happily ever after." We had friendship, deep love, and, though we didn't really know about a personal relationship with Christ, we did somehow believe that God had brought us together.

Instead of what should have been, after eight years our marriage was in ruins. What happened? There were lots of things that went wrong, but the root was pretty simple: we never put Christ at our center. That changed for me when David left for an affair with a co-worker. I was devastated; in my rock bottom condition, I finally turned to God seriously, and on August 13, 1977, I was officially born again.

Immediately I began to pray for David because my deepest desire was that he would also have spiritual transformation. It was one of the worst times in my life, but it was also one of the best times because of how tightly I locked into God.

Practically speaking, I had to get a job, find new housing, and raise two small daughters; but no matter what I did, I was always praying. Always. I found and claimed every promise from God's Word that pertained to us and constantly declared them over our lives. When I realized the power of fasting, it was added on a regular basis. I spared absolutely nothing in my pursuit of David being saved to the uttermost. I also believed that once the light turned on for him, he would return to the covenant commitment he made on our wedding day.

One day I was driving home from work and just rounding a corner. I wasn't thinking about anything in particular when suddenly the dream about Vietnam and the foxhole popped into my head. Wow. That was a long time ago, and why was I remembering it now? As I mulled it over, I had one of those "Aha" moments. I understood the dream.

David was without spiritual hearing in his "right" ear—the ear where you hear "right" from wrong. There was a battle going on for his soul. I was in the battle *with* him and *for* him, but God was giving me a choice just like the military did in the dream: I didn't have to stay. It seemed like God was asking me whether I was willing to, and he wouldn't hold it against me if I didn't.

Remembering how fierce the battle was in the dream, I knew if I said yes it would be a very tough fight. Yet I had no hesitation, especially now that I realized God had given advance notice to me that it would come to this. And really, I had started the spiritual battle already anyhow. I was also struck by God's deep interest and caring for David. His soul was worth the fight, as God had partnered him with a very scrappy wife.

I understood the dream, but I didn't know what the outcome would be. Over many years, I fought with everything in me but saw no results. Just as a long time elapsed between having the dream and knowing its meaning, it would be over thirty more years before I knew who won the war for David's soul.

Rule Number One

What can my own Vietnam dream teach you about how to interpret dreams in general? Lots. The most important rule in interpreting your own dream is answering this question: what did the dream mean to *you?* You may say, "Well, if I knew that, I wouldn't need help with the interpretation." What I am saying is to trust yourself as you separate the elements in the dream and analyze the associated symbols and emotions.

The dream came to *you* and you have within yourself the best ability to understand what those particular elements mean. There are classic, common dream symbols, but they may not fit your dream and you shouldn't try to force them. Interpret out of your own well of understanding before going to standard symbol meanings.

My dream came out of the well of understanding that I already had about my natural world at that time. It used current events of the day and my current situation in life to convey what might have simply been a scary dream about being in a war zone. Yet all these elements pointed to spiritual equivalents that I wasn't capable of understanding then. Isn't God smart? He used what I *could* understand to lay a foundation for true understanding later.

What the dream meant to me when I originally had it was that if David were ever in mortal danger, I would stick with him even if it meant I would also be in danger. And if I could opt out of the danger for myself, I would not do it. The strength of the emotions in the dream showed me that.

Emotions

The particular emotions you feel in a dream and the strength of those emotions tell you, almost more than anything else, about what the dream means. The overriding emotions are more important than the events or their sequence, so ask yourself what you really felt. This could be easier said than done. Suppose you feel scared. Yes, but is there an emotion underlying that? Why do you feel scared? What are you afraid is going to happen? Asking yourself questions is the best way to get at it. The answers may provide the correct interpretation.

In my case, even though there was great fear, the overriding emotion was dread. With all my heart I didn't want to be there. That's why I could be so sure that I would stick through it even if I could leave. Because in the dream, I did stay, when I was free to go at any time. And, ultimately, it was still my choice when I understood the dream was actually about spiritual warfare, not the war in Vietnam.

Of all the dreams people send me, very rarely do they relay the emotions of the dream. For instance, here's one that I received many years ago. It said, "My wife has been having dreams about spiders and snakes. They have been biting her. The snakes bite her on the arms and the spiders on the feet. I have read that means she is going to be under the attack of evil. Is that true?" Well, I have no idea. Dreams don't occur in a vacuum. What is going on in the wife's natural world? What does she feel in the dreams? How strongly does she feel it?

If one emotion plays out over and over but in different dreams over time, it's worth keeping track of and examining more closely. In this case, the dreamer may be working through a deep life issue; if so, when the issue is resolved, the dreams will change or stop.

Details

Details of the dream are only important if they stand out to the dreamer. In my dream, let's look at the "ear." Of course an ear would generally represent hearing, and my dream drew from the well of understanding that I already had about David's hearing impairment. It was the hearing of his right ear that was nearly gone. When I woke up from the dream, the detail stood out to me because it was why I was allowed to stay in the foxhole with him even though I had not been drafted to active duty. But later, I came to understand that this was an important detail in the interpretation, though with a different meaning of the word "right" as I mentioned earlier.

The school bus dream I related in Chapter 2 provides another example of the importance of details. It kept nagging at me to wonder why he was in the first row, while I was in the second. The whole interpretation actually hinged on that detail. So, as I said before, if a detail bothers you, for whatever reason, pay attention to it. But all those other random details that just seem to float by for no reason at all, chalk them up to the general disarray of the dream world itself. You can probably safely dismiss them.

Symbols

While God does sometimes speak directly in dreams, more often than not there are symbols to interpret. Think about Daniel who served the Babylonian king, Nebuchadnezzar. In the first instance, he actually had to tell the king what he had dreamed before telling him the interpretation. He did so with exquisite humility when he said, *"But as for me, this mystery has not been revealed to me for any wisdom residing in me more than in any other living man, but for the purpose of making the interpretation known to the king, and that you may understand the thoughts of your mind"* (Daniel 2:30).

In the dream there was a statue, and the head was gold. Daniel told the king, *"You are the head of gold"* (Daniel 2:38b). He proceeded to explain each symbol in the dream with simplicity and ease. I wish it were as easy for us, but Daniel had a special gift and special anointing. Still, the more we practice, the more we will grow in interpreting our dreams' symbols.

First, look for the common meaning of a symbol or the special meaning it has to you or your family. For instance, suppose you see the numbers 743 flashing in stark white against a black background as part of your dream. After you awake, you know that detail is important, and you wonder what it means. Upon reflection, you remember that 743 was the house number of your family home when you were a child. Ah, now you are on to a key for your interpretation.

If a symbol has no particular meaning for you, look for the common meaning it has within your culture. For instance, a fox is sly and cunning; a bed represents rest or it might mean intimacy; and a beard is associated with old age and perhaps wisdom. This is where a generic dream symbol dictionary can come in handy as long as you use it carefully and don't take it to be infallible. Simply looking up each item in the dictionary will not necessarily give you the correct interpretation. Don't forget *Rule Number One:*

*what did the dream mean to **you**.* Still, it can sometimes give you clues.

Dream Elements

Perhaps we can pull a lot of these guidelines together by breaking down dreams through the elements that make them up. Someone once sent me an interesting dream about a bridge, asking for help in understanding its meaning. I couldn't really interpret the dream, especially without knowing him or his situation personally. So how could I help him come to the best conclusions and the correct interpretation? Read the dream and my take on it. Hopefully, it can serve as a model for some of the dreams you might like to interpret.

The Bridge Dream

> *I dreamed I was getting ready to walk over a bridge. Before we set out, my wife said, "Are you sure that you are ready to do this? There are a lot of things out there." Along the way, certain parts of the bridge didn't have guardrails that were very high and the bridge was very high in the air. Beneath it was a beautiful blue lake, and at certain stages I could see the bottom that had rocks or pebbles at the bottom. I almost fell off of the bridge, but held onto one of the guardrails and was able to get back on. My family was with me in this dream.*

We first ask, what is the central theme of the dream? Some dreams are confused and multifaceted, but in this case it is simple: a bridge and a journey across it. Always try initially to remove as many elements and details as possible from the dream in order to bring it down to its simplest form, and then attempt to interpret *that*.

Bridges are often symbolic of faith, trials, a way or path, or even joining two things together. Now think: Is that what a bridge means to *you*? Does the general interpretation feel solid, or do bridges have a particular meaning in your life or family? Go first with the personal meaning of the element before applying the general meaning.

Now it is time to add details. Why do certain details show up in a dream and not others? Because those are the important ones, so pay attention! This dreamer did not see what was at the other side of the bridge. That may indicate the dream is about the process of crossing, not the end result.

There were guardrails on the bridge, which may indicate safety or protection on the journey, but sometimes they were missing or not very high, which may represent danger. Indeed, a warning was called out by the dreamer's wife: "Are you sure you want to do this?" That may represent choice in the matter. If this is a dream about a walk of faith or trial in the offing, the dreamer may have options before beginning it.

Detail by detail; use good old common sense in evaluating what each might mean. Also, it is significant who is in the dream, and even who isn't. For instance, this dreamer had his wife and family along. Does that represent support and help during a coming trial? If he would have been alone, that might have been significant as well, indicating going it alone.

After reviewing the central theme, all the details, and who was included in the dream, it is time to step back and ask yourself how you felt—both during the dream and afterward. As stated earlier, the emotions of a dream are probably the most significant elements, and are most often overlooked. In this case, the dreamer didn't say. But he must ask: Was I scared or confident. Was I excited to start off or filled with self-doubt? Was I relieved to wake up or did I enjoy the dream?

Three years after my correspondence with the bridge dreamer, I received a follow-up. He wrote and told me that he had been deployed in Iraq when he had the dream, but that deployment was interrupted when a brain tumor was discovered. So the dream was foreshadowing a coming trial. He states, "After three hospitals and lots of healing, it is gone. During this period of my life, my wife and kids were there every step of the way. Thank you for all of the help you gave me in understanding this dream."

Dream Journal

Keeping a dream journal can be of much value over time. However, in order to keep the journal, it is first necessary to remember your dreams, and some people have greater difficulty with this than others. Usually, though, by putting a little attention on it, it can be turned around successfully. Awaking naturally helps. Try spending a few quiet moments asking yourself if there isn't at least some little snippet of a dream that comes to mind. Write it down, and don't forget to date it.

As the weeks and months slip by, you will key into your dream world with greater ease. You may begin eventually to pick up patterns or repeated symbols in your dreams. Read back through the journal occasionally to see what strikes you. Keep a pencil handy, and write notes and questions to yourself about the dreams. "Why does my sister always wear blue in my dreams?" "Why didn't I care in this dream that my husband was leaving on a trip without me?" Note that if you are in the dream, it is probably about you, so ask if you are a participant or observer in the dream.

Suppose you are not a person who has any trouble remembering your dreams. Rather, you easily remember your dreams in great detail. Keeping a journal will be easier for you, but it may become pretty cumbersome. Too much! Then don't write down every single detail but just summarize, and notate only the details and symbols that strike you as significant.

The vast majority of dreams that go into a journal will be of the "soulish" variety. These are the bread-and-butter dreams that come out of your subconscious longings, fears, hopes, etc. Writing them down gives you a window into your soul, and that can be valuable for lots of reasons. It lets you know what is going on under the surface, and may point to areas where you need counseling of some type or special prayer.

The dream journal also accentuates an out-of-the-ordinary dream. It will be much easier to determine dream origins if you are used to remembering and writing down your dreams.

If possible, share your dreams with someone. As I mentioned in the Introduction, when I was a child we regularly told our dreams around the breakfast table. I don't know why we did that, but it was fun, and we particularly liked to hear about our mother's dreams because those were the most intriguing. Talking about dreams is another way to stir the pot and get the dream juices flowing.

Prayer

I leave the best, and most important help, for last. What about God and the dream? What is *He* saying, if anything? "Lord, did this dream come from You? What does it mean? What should I do with it? Please help me understand." You may not get an immediate answer, and you may have to put the dream up on a shelf for a time, but if He gave you the dream, it will become clear eventually. Never omit this final step, because His answer is the only one that really matters.

CHAPTER 4

Common Subjects of Dreams

Based on my mail, certain subjects come up over and over in people's dreams. Perhaps discussion of some of the ones I've noticed most will aid in interpretation in general. Often the origin of these common dreams is the soulish realm, but even so, it doesn't preclude God's hand working through them. And no matter where they come from, we still want to know why we dreamed them and what they mean in our lives.

Death Dreams

What does it mean to dream, either repeatedly or for the first time, about people who have died? First, let's think about all the things that death can mean: finality, separation, estrangement, dissolution, decay, permanence, parting, irrevocable finish, afterlife, loss, release, bereavement, end of life. I used quite a few possibilities (and I could certainly have used many more) in order to demonstrate that death in a dream may have an interpretation other than physical death.

Here are two sample dreams that can be viewed from entirely different perspectives.

> *Since my mother passed away six months ago, I've had recurring dreams of her funeral. This is, to say the least, very disturbing. Please help me with this if you can.* —C

> *I never have dreamed about my father who died 15 years ago, and yesterday I dreamed that he was sitting on a chair in a grey suit with dark sunglasses. When I went up to touch him his head fell off and I yelled, "Dad is dead, tell somebody!" I am so confused as to what this can mean. Please help me...I am going through a divorce currently.* —J

Even though these dreams are different, there are some noteworthy commonalities. Both are about a parent who is now deceased. In one, the mother died fairly recently; in the other, the subject is a father who died more than a decade ago. How do we therefore approach interpretation?

In C's dream, it is important to keep in mind the mother's recent death, which probably plays a major role in why the dream is recurring. It is not uncommon to work through the grief process at least partially while dreaming. This is not a concern because eventually it will work itself out and the dreams will stop. Still, there is an important question to ask: exactly *what* is being worked through?

My questions for C: are there any unresolved issues between you and your mom? This is not a comforting dream; it is one that is "very disturbing." The emotions attached to the dream are extremely important and should be noted. Is there frustration or anger or unforgiveness or other emotions within the dream itself? All of these things are clues.

For J, an important clue is her ending disclosure that she is currently going through a divorce. This is not part of the normal grief process for her dad, since the death was so long ago and because it is the first dream she has had about it. I do believe it probable, however, that there is a different kind of grief involved.

My question for J: what elements of your relationship with your father exist in your relationship with your husband? Since you are going through a divorce and that relationship is being "beheaded" or "lopped" off, it is worth asking yourself if you feel that you are losing a father again.

In the case of the first dream, the events of the past are encroaching on the present and bringing a recurring dream. In the second case, current events are reaching back to a relationship that ended fifteen years ago.

Fortunately, I had additional correspondence with both of these dreamers, so I was able to confirm that my questioning hit the mark both times. Both of them actually had an innate sense of the real meaning of their dreams but needed some nudging to be reminded that they knew the truth all along. This is often the case. Ask yourself a lot of questions about the dream and then remember to trust your gut!

What if you dream that someone is going to die? Yes, the possibility exists that you are receiving a warning dream and you'll need to really pray for discernment on how to proceed. There may be other explanations, however. Does fear play any role in the dream? For instance, a mother dreams that her only child dies, but when she deeply examines herself, she realizes she has always been afraid that if she really loves something, God will take it away from her. So then the dream is more about her relationship with God than about death.

As you examine your own unique death dreams, use the definitions or synonyms I mentioned above to see what resonates with you. Think about the elements in your own life or environment that may have triggered the dream. Death of a relationship? Release from something that needs to die? Working through the emotions of bereavement? Fear of death and eternity? Facing something in your life that is final? Ask, did the dream bring peace or confusion? Did it make you sad or happy? As always, what details seem most important?

Marriage Partner Dreams

These dreams should come with a big BEWARE sign etched on a big red flag. In other words, don't trust them! I have received hundreds of emails from people who actually married someone based on a dream. After disastrous results, they say they don't understand God's purposes.

Often the dreams are before the fact and people wonder if they should marry the person they keep dreaming about. Sometimes the dream is about an old flame and they have recurring dreams about getting back together. Sometimes it is a Christian wondering if it is okay to marry an unbeliever because the dream indicates it. (That would be a *no*, by the way.)

Usually, in this type of dream, there is an enormous attraction to a particular person, and the dream acts as a confirmation. That's the major problem with dreams relating to whom we should marry. Our flesh has too strong a foothold. It is too easy to hear what we want to hear.

I will acknowledge that there are probably a few people out there who dreamed prophetically about a person they were going to marry and all turned out well. Even so, I also believe that these cases are rare compared to the number of people who have this type of dream out of their fleshly desires. So rather than try to interpret them, let's talk about how to handle them with wisdom.

Some suggestions:

- Treat this type of dream with suspicion.

- Do not act on the dream; let God unfold His purposes for marriage without any manipulation on your part.

- Make sure no biblical instructions regarding marriage are violated (e.g., the person is already married to someone else or the person is a non-believer or the person is not living a godly life, etc.).

Sexual Dreams

Dreams with sexual content are very common and, if my mail is correct, they are often embarrassing and guilt provoking. Here's a sample:

> *I sometimes have dreams where I am having sex, sometimes with people I know and sometimes with people I don't know. I am concerned because I take authority over my dreams but I still have those dreams. I don't understand the dream and I don't know why it won't go away.* –T

If you have sexual dreams similar to this, I begin by encouraging you. One place you get a "free pass" from guilt is in your dreams. You can control your thought life and you can control your actions (as you must), but you cannot control what you dream. The exception to this would be to control any activity in your waking hours that would heighten sexual interest, such as images or TV shows or music with a predominantly sexual theme. Such materials could fuel a fire that plays out while you sleep.

Most sexual dreams, however, have a very simple explanation. The dreamer needs to ask if, at this juncture in life, they are sexually frustrated. The sex drive is normal and natural, but if you are not married and have no legitimate sexual outlet, this may be the body's back-up plan. And, even if married, depending on many factors, there may be frustrations that are playing out in the dream world.

There is also a second way to look at dreams with sexual content. Sometimes sex in a dream represents intimacy and has nothing to do with sex itself. Therefore, if a person dreams of sex with their brother, it doesn't necessarily mean that there is a sexual attraction to the brother; it may mean there is a growing closeness or a desire for greater closeness. The context of the dreamer's waking life should help with navigation to the correct interpretation.

Other People's Dreams

Please help me. I am very troubled by what a work colleague told me. She said she had a dream in which she and I were walking together and a vicious dog approached. She became very afraid of the dog but I laughed and assured her that the dog would not bite. However the dog did actually bite her despite my assurances. —N

Should N be concerned because she shows up in her co-worker's dream? Not really. Dream language is extremely personal and subjective, and most dreams are for the dreamer alone. The exception is a prophetic dream that

God gives someone for the church or for a particular group or even one person.

The interpretation of the dream depends on the perspective of the dreamer. Sometimes the appearance of a person in a dream is only a prop for the dreamer who has to determine the meaning of that prop. Let's consider some likely interpretations for this particular dream.

For the co-worker, the dream may speak to her relationship with N, and may point to several possibilities. In her heart she may see N as braver or more courageous than herself. Or she may feel N's judgment is not trustworthy, because she sees N as too trusting and naïve. In the dream, N was not right about the dog. The dog could represent any perceived danger in the workplace.

Is there ever a time when we should pay attention if we show up in someone else's dream? Yes, there might be a few cases, so ask yourself the following questions: Does the dreamer have a gift of prophecy and a track record of accurate dreams? Does the dream seem to have nothing to do with their life—only yours? Is the dream reoccurring? Does the dream have a special quality about it that the dreamer senses has relevance for you? Does the hearing of the dream strike some deep chord and give you a feeling of "this is for me"?

If none of these questions can be answered in the affirmative, the dream was no doubt meant only for the one who dreamed it. You can dismiss it and go back to puzzling over your own dreams.

Attack Dreams

Who hasn't dreamed at one time or another that a vicious animal or ominous stranger is attacking them? Sometimes we are desperately running from attack, even while losing ground. Often we wake up just before the bear, or whatever, nabs us. The timely wake up is no doubt a survival mechanism since the dream feels so real.

Since the most common emotions in such dreams are fear and panic, let's examine interpretations based on that. What is going on in your life that is overwhelming? That you fear you can't get away from? That is out of your control?

For instance, a person going through financial struggles may have such a dream because of the fear of ruin. If we are afraid someone in our workplace is an enemy, this fear may play out in an attack dream. If it is difficult to determine the roots of our fear, we need the help of the Holy Spirit to shine a light on the underlying causes. Sometimes a dream detail that seems important may point to a correct interpretation. Don't forget to pray and then wait with expectation that understanding will come.

House Dreams

When you dream of a house, you are almost always dreaming of something in your own life, even if the house in the dream isn't yours. Once I came to that realization, it made interpretation of my own dreams much easier. Here's something else: dreams occurring in the back yard often represent your past. I've personally had a very strong dream like that. It may also be true that dreams in the front yard refer to your future (worth considering), but I haven't had any personal experiences to cite in this case so I'm not sure.

Bathroom Dreams

When you dream about needing a restroom, yet every one you come upon is either filthy dirty or there is no privacy, what is really going on? People often interpret these types of dreams as having to do with needing to "purge" or "eliminate" something. These are possibilities worth considering. Do you feel "dirty" about something? Do you want to get rid of something but don't want it publicly known?

If the answer is no, there may be a more natural explanation for the dream. Possibly you actually need to use the bathroom in the middle of the night but, since you are asleep, the normal cues don't work. Your dream world takes over and you dream about finding a place to go but of course never feel relief (going from restroom to restroom in the dream). Finally, as the urgency becomes greater, you struggle from slumber to enough consciousness to get up.

All of the dreams I've mentioned here are commonplace. How many of them do you identify with? Perhaps a few, yet you probably also have many dreams that don't fit into any of these categories; they are unique to you. In the next chapter, we will look at some real dreams from real people and see if any of them can aid you further in interpreting your own dreams.

CHAPTER 5

Real Dreams, Real People

Let's examine some real dreams from real people, to aid you as you puzzle over your own unique dreams. In some cases, these dreams were submitted to me by people I don't know personally, so I will be speculating on the correct interpretation. I'm including them to show you the questioning process. Learn to ask the right questions about your dreams because good questions produce good interpretations!

Other dreams in this chapter are from my friends and family, and in those cases, the correct interpretation is pretty well-known for various reasons. Hopefully, there is enough of a sampling of different kinds of dreams to further you in your own deciphering.

Pearls and Wrinkles Dream

I dreamed that my husband had died (though he wasn't in the dream) and I was trying to get to my sons to find out if anyone had told them. After I talked to my first son, I asked where my other son was and I finally came upon him reclining on a couch. I asked if he knew and he did. As I went to him, he raised his arms to comfort and embrace me, and I noticed that his arms were terribly wrinkled and sagging. Also, he had an old-fashioned set of pearls around his neck. In the dream I thought how strange that was; and after I woke up, I continued to wonder about those two details. After all, my son is a strong man in quite good shape. And where did the pearls come from? The main emotion of the dream was comfort. —S

When my friend had this dream, she realized that seeking her younger son if her husband died would be most natural because of their extremely close relationship. They have very similar temperaments and her son seems to "get her" better than almost anybody. The biggest question she had was why her son looked so odd, with wrinkled arms, when the rest of him looked normal, and the pearls he wore. So she asked God and He told her. "Because you have always seen your son like a mother to you. Those symbols remind you of your own mother." So true, she thought. In the end of her life, her mother's arms looked just like that, and she always wore the same kind of big costume pearls.

My friend did the smart thing and put her questions to God first. Without any struggling at all, she had her interpretation regarding the details that stumped her. Submitting your dreams to God is always the best first choice, though I will readily admit that S often gets her answers much faster than many of us.

Secret Rooms Dream

> *Could you tell me what secret rooms mean? Or rooms in a house that you didn't know were there? I have had many dreams over the years where I will come into my house (quite large houses in different dreams) only to walk around and find more passageways to various wings and sections of the house. All of them are beautiful and high class. I always wanted to use the rooms but never did in my dreams. —R*

This dream came to me from a woman I do not know, so I will have to approach it differently. I never had any follow-up communication and we are therefore left with speculation. Still, I do know that dreaming of a house is a strong indicator of dreaming of your own life. With that in mind, we can ask some pertinent questions.

- If this is your life, are there portions of it you feel are unused or unexplored?

- Do you suspect you have gifts and talents that are somewhere in you, but hidden?

- Is there anything that is hindering you from the life you wish you could have? For instance, do you somehow feel you missed your career calling, and now it is too late?

- Are you a "mystery" to yourself? Perhaps you don't feel you really know who you are at the root?

If the dreamer identifies with any of these things, the next step is to decide if there is a need to work through a condition of the soul, or if God is prompting a challenge to discover the hidden rooms. Maybe some of them can still be opened up. And, I can assure R that once the root is worked through, the dreams will change or stop.

The Orchid/Obama Dream

> *I'm writing to ask if you have any information about the symbolism of an orchid or its meaning. I had a dream—it was strong and comforting, in which Robert Gibbs (President Obama's press secretary) offered me a piece of cake as a gift of gratitude for all I do behind the scenes. It was presented on a sterling silver platter. What puzzles me is that I would not have chosen that dessert from the platter, but he said this one was especially created for me. There was an orchid of the most extraordinarily delicate beauty I'd ever seen in the traditional orchid color, draped over the sides of the triangular piece of cake.*

> *I've been called to intercede for Obama starting many months in advance of his election—to the ire of most all my friends, three of whom it appears I've lost forever. They refuse to pray or communicate*

with me any longer. Still, I've remained steadfast
in this call. –B

I don't normally interpret dreams for other people; I'd rather teach them how to interpret their dreams for themselves. Occasionally, however, I hear a dream and I just "know"—at least certain pieces of it. In this dream, the element of the orchid really struck me.

Part of my answer to B was this: "First, I do believe this is a prophetic dream from God confirming to you your call to pray for the president. As to the orchid, I think you should consider that an orchid was used, not because of symbolism of orchids, but because President Obama was born in Hawaii and that is a commonly grown flower there. Orchids are grown all around the world, but Hawaii is prominent in growing and exporting them. Remember that they 'exported' Obama to the mainland."

Here are some additional questions to be asked to probe more nuggets of meaning:

- Does "for all you do behind the scenes" refer to the special prayer you have been called to, which will mostly be done in the secret prayer closet?

- It's not the dessert you would have chosen— perhaps this call is not what you would have chosen for yourself?

- Cake is sweet, so is it a promise that the prayer will be satisfying?

- Why was the cake triangular? Perhaps you are asked to pray for three years? (Think about the meaning of three.) Or, does this refer to the three lost friends—the price to pay for obeying the Lord's call?

Why did I see this as a prophetic dream? It doesn't appear to have anything to do with B's own life in the sense of anything she needs to work through, and we already know that she feels God called her to this special assignment. The dream was comforting, so it appears to confirm that assignment. Another thing to note is that the dream was fairly simple and did not include a lot of random images unrelated to the subject of the dream. This lady realized the dream had to do with her call; she simply needed help with some of the symbols.

She's Trying to Kill Me Dream

The following was the reoccurring dream of a nine-year-old boy who is now thirteen. He repeatedly dreamed that an aunt was trying to kill him. She would get him into a private place and proceed to either attempt to smother him, or use a knife to stab him. He would always just barely get away, and then try to find his mother or father to tell them. The worst part of the dream was that neither parent seemed to care. They acted disinterested when he begged for help.

Warning dream? Demonic dream? Neither. There is context to this dream without which it really can't be interpreted correctly. At the time the dreams were happening, this young man's parents were getting divorced. I talked to him four years afterward and the dreams had stopped. I listened to the dream and then asked him what he thought it meant. "I think it was because of the divorce," he said. I agreed. Even at his young age, he could interpret his dream with wisdom.

We talked it over and he remembers that at the time of the divorce, he didn't feel anyone was paying attention to what was happening to him. Like, "I'm being killed here and you don't care!" There were multiple emotions to process, and his dream world helped him work them through.

This dream demonstrates the necessity of examining the context of your life rather than just grabbing a dream symbol dictionary and trying to force a meaning.

Romantic Husband Dream

> *I was told this dream in a casual encounter and we never discussed the interpretation, so I'm not sure if E would agree with the one I came to after pondering it. For years she has had dreams in which her husband is intensely romantic. They are wonderful dreams, but what doesn't make sense for her is that being "romantic" is the complete opposite of what her husband is really like. She*

said, "That's not him AT ALL" and is puzzled about why she would dream that he is.

I have a hunch that even though E's husband isn't the romantic type, she *is!* I would ask her that question if we were together again talking about this dream. I think she's dreaming about her own desire for such displays from her husband. Since that's not unusual at all, I thought it was worth including an example. Perhaps we could call them "surrogate" dreams in which other people (friends, family, spouses) take on emotions or actions that really represent ourselves. It's worth considering the next time your dream includes someone you know acting out of character.

False Friend Dream

I was in 6th grade (12 years old) when this dream occurred. In the dream, I was standing in the street out in front of my house, talking to a person. I did not recognize the person as someone I knew in my awake life, but in the dream, I knew that the person was my friend. The person reached out and grabbed my hand to shake it, and was smiling as though it was a friendly thing. But somehow I knew, even though I couldn't see it, that the person's other hand was behind his/her back clenched into a fist, and the person wanted to punch me. I woke with an unsettled, somewhat shocked feeling.

I told my mom about the dream that morning, and then didn't really think about it.

A few weeks later, I was playing with a girl who was my best friend at school. It was twilight and dusky. I told her that I needed to go home, but she wanted me to come back to her house for some reason. I started to walk away and stepped into the street, and she reached out and grabbed my hand to pull me back toward her house. I pulled away from her and said I had to go home.

When I went to school the next day, she wouldn't talk to me, and had rallied several kids to be on her side and not talk to me as well. When I told my mom about it later that day, she reminded me of the dream I had had, because she thought that the Lord was warning me about this girl.

After a few days, the girl and her posse started talking to me again, but over the course of the next year, several things happened to really make it clear to me that though she was acting like my friend, she actually wasn't.

Crazily enough, some thirty years later, she sent me a friend request on Facebook. I did not accept. –J

I've included this warning dream primarily for two reasons. The first is, don't dismiss the dreams of children. Rather, listen to them carefully, and with interest, because they just might be important. Second, I'd like to again highlight how valuable it is to share dreams. This dreamer's mother was able to provide beneficial feedback, and perhaps protected J from things we'll never know about because they didn't happen.

Jesus on the Roof Dream

When I was about 23 I had this dream. At the time, I was dating the man who would become my husband, and I found out after the dream that he had been praying for me. I had been raised Lutheran and my idea of God was that He was completely unapproachable. A girlfriend named Julie had been telling me about a personal relationship with Christ and a part of me wanted what she had. Yet, I just wouldn't do anything about it.

One night I dreamed that I was at a regular, old-fashioned summer camp. Every detail of the campus, the dining hall, and the cabins is as clear to me today as it was then, over twenty years later. We were all in the dining hall for the evening meal when the sky turned the blackest black you could imagine and a huge wind started up. Debris was blowing all over the place. We were sent running to our assigned cabins to pull the shutters and secure the place. I started to pull the shutters on the front window when an enormously loud BANG went off on the roof. I thought it must be a very large tree fallen.

*I ran out on the porch and looked up to see what had happened but it was no tree. Instead, there was Jesus, bigger than life, and the storm was raging around Him, and the wind was whipping at His white clothes. He looked straight into my eyes with great intensity and said, "**I need to speak to you!**" Then I woke up. –M*

I asked M how she felt when she woke up. She said she felt slightly breathless as if she had been in a real storm, but she felt absolutely no fear. I also asked about the main emotions of the dream. "I felt a little bit ashamed, or maybe embarrassed. You know, that the Lord had to go to such lengths to grab my attention. I hadn't been paying attention to all the signs He had been sending me, especially through my friend Julie. But that did it for me. Two days later Julie led me through the sinner's prayer."

What a powerful prophetic dream, one that needs no extra interpretation. The message to the dreamer was crystal clear. I was really taken aback when M told me that another friend at the time tried to get her to dismiss the dream. She told her that God doesn't speak in dreams anymore today—that they were only something that happened back in Bible times. But M was the one who had the dream and she knew better. Her heart was changed by it, and she considers that dream the most pivotal moment of her spiritual life.

I've said it often in these pages, so I guess I can say it one more time. *You* are the dreamer, and *you* are best able to interpret your own dreams. Yes, some guidelines are needed, and some godly wisdom. Don't forget prayer. Be decidedly honest with yourself in evaluating your dreams, especially those that most probably come from the soulish realm. But after all of that, trust your gut!

Next, we will be looking at some classic dream symbols. They shouldn't be used like a fast food drive-thru; rather, they can suggest possibilities to ponder as you resolve the origins and meanings of your dreams.

CHAPTER 6

Dream Symbols

While we will be examining a few classic dream symbols in this chapter, it is not my intention to provide an exhaustive list. Rather, I'd like to recommend ways to develop your own personal dream dictionary and to determine the meaning of a particular symbol in your dream for yourself.

I do highly recommend a book that is not really intended for dreams per se, but is the best one I know of for accuracy and completeness of symbols and types found in the Bible. It is called *Interpreting the Symbols and Types* by Kevin J. Conner. I cannot match his research, nor would I be wise to try. I keep this little volume handy at all times, and it has helped me with my dreams more often than I can say.

Developing Your Own Dream Dictionary

Previously, I have suggested keeping a dream journal so that over time you can pick up recurring themes. It might also be valuable for you to keep a running list of symbols that show up in your dreams. This is different from the journal because you are simply jotting down the symbols without the dream narrative. For instance:

- Bear
- Full moon
- The color blue
- Lighthouse
- Five-dollar bills
- Turnpikes
- Police
- Sail boat
- Earthquake

You might put a date behind the symbol each time it occurs, which will help with establishing a track record for reoccurring themes. I don't suggest writing down every detail of the dream as a symbol, just the ones that seem significant to you.

Suppose, then, that you have had three or four dreams in which an earthquake played a central role, yet each dream was uniquely different. How do you interpret that symbol for yourself? Classically, earthquakes represent upheaval, change by crisis, a trial, disaster, trauma, and the judgments of God. Remember what happened as Jesus yielded His Spirit on the cross: *"And behold, the veil of the temple was torn in two from top to bottom; and the earth shook and the rocks were split"* (Matthew 27:51).

Earthquakes also play heavily in the end time judgments: *"I looked when He broke the sixth seal, and there was a great earthquake; and the sun became black as sackcloth made of hair, and the whole moon became like blood"* (Revelation 6:12).

So why are you dreaming of earthquakes? Perhaps the most natural explanation for you is that you live near a fault line and you experience actual earthquakes all the time. During the night there is a slight vibration and your subconscious picks it up and incorporates it into your dream. A good rule of thumb is to start with the simplest explanation first. No, you say, I don't live in a region where earthquakes are common. Okay, let's keep looking. How does the earthquake affect you in the dream? Are you afraid? Who else is there with you? What is the outcome? Now, try to tie the answers to these questions to the current events of your life at the time of the dream.

Maybe you realize that, for the past couple of years, your life has been in constant upheaval. Nothing seems stable and the only thing that seems constant is change. Maybe it feels like you are being shaken down to your core. Or perhaps you are trying desperately to shake loose from an addiction, and your dream reflects that.

On another level, what if you are not a participant in the earthquake dream, but an observer? It might be a prophetic dream. A man once wrote me about a dream that took place inside his church. He watched while an earth-quake occurred as the congregation sat in the pews. He wondered if his church was in for a great shaking, and I bet he was right.

Symbols that Contradict

Some classic dream symbols seem to contradict themselves. Since they can mean opposite things, how do you interpret them? For instance, what will a classic dream dictionary tell you about *nudity?* One may list "impure" and "ashamed," while another says "truth" and "honest" and "innocent." If you use the dictionary without context, you may end up confused.

Actually, nudity can represent all of the things above. For instance, Adam and Eve were naked in the Garden of Eden—they were completely innocent and honest before God. But what happened after they ate the fruit that was forbidden to them? *"Then the eyes of both of them were opened, and they knew that they were naked; and they sewed fig leaves together and made themselves loin coverings"* (Genesis 3:7). Now they were impure and ashamed. Within the contents of one story we have both meanings.

Another symbol that can be taken two (or even three or more) ways is *lion.* In Scripture, Jesus is the Lion of Judah: *"and one of the elders said to me, 'Stop weeping; behold, the Lion that is from the tribe of Judah, the Root of David, has overcome so as to open the book and its seven seals"* (Revelation 5:5). Yet, the anti-Christ is also seen as a "lion" a few chapters later:

"And the beast which I saw was like a leopard, and his feet were like those of bear, and his mouth like the mouth of a lion. And the dragon gave him his power and his throne and great authority" (Revelation 13:2). Both lions, however, represent kingship and authority. (Good to know that in the end of natural history, King Jesus takes full authority over the anti-Christ and He *wins* for all eternity!)

There are three important things to remember about choosing a meaning for your dream symbol:

1. Start with the simplest and most natural possibility first (like my earthquake example).

2. Use the common meanings of things within your own cultural context (e.g., an eagle for an American often represents patriotism or courage because it is a national symbol).

3. Keep the symbol in sync with the context of the dream. For instance, a wolf is associated with Satan and evil or false ministries; but if your dream is about your favorite stuffed toy wolf from childhood, any interpretation connoting evil is probably out of place.

The following are symbols and common meanings I have found true throughout the more than 30 years I have been studying dreams and their meanings. You may find that my list matches or closely resembles other dream dictionaries including Conner's, which I mentioned previously. That's because there is a universal understanding about various classic symbols such as these.

Classic Colors

White: Purity, righteousness, holiness

Black: Death, famine, a void, unable to see, as in the inky blackness of night

Yellow: Cowardice (yellow-bellied), fear or timidity, but also caution, slow down (think of the yellow traffic light)

Red: Sacrifice (blood of Christ for our sin), suffering; also, anger or rage (seeing "red" or being in the red zone, out of control)

Blue: Heaven or heavenly authority, restfulness

Green: Rest (lying down in green pastures), hope, prosperity (typical color of money), growth, life

Purple: Royalty, wealth, prosperity

Orange: Danger, jeopardy, beware (the color of orange barrels during highway repairs)

Seasons

Spring: Renewal, begin again, revival, regeneration, salvation, refreshing

Summer: Heat of affliction, growing to maturity

Autumn: Harvest time, reaping, beginning of decay, prep for the hard times, change on the way

Winter: Barrenness, dormant season, coldness (may be natural or spiritual), unfriendly, bitter; could also be the "hidden" season when activity is unseen for a time

Classic Activities in Dreams

Falling: Loss of something, free-falling as in having no control, fear of crashing, or hitting bottom

Flying: Excitement, freedom, exhilarating, having no limits, without encumbrances

Running naked in public view: Fear of exposure

Garden scenes: Productive activity, growth, nurturing, symbol of fertility

Riding in various conveyances: Plane, train, automobile, boat, etc., going somewhere or getting somewhere in life; depending on activity, may represent the hardship of the trip or smooth sailing

Drowning: Feeling overwhelmed, experiencing grief or sorrow, having excessive debt, may reveal self-pity

Fire: Could represent the presence of God or might represent being purified or tested

Kissing: Covenant agreement, romance, desire fulfilled; or on the flip side, Jesus was betrayed with a kiss so it could also mean deception or seduction by a friend

Pregnancy: In process, anticipation, expectancy that something will be born in due time such as a dream or ministry; waiting for right time

I know I haven't even scratched the surface in the few symbols I have handled above. Again, this is in keeping with my basic philosophy of trusting yourself over a book. There are many dream symbol dictionaries out there, and some of them may be worthwhile in getting your interpretive juices flowing. The one I mentioned earlier, *Interpreting the Symbols and Types,* is most certainly worthwhile. Yet, regarding dream interpretation, a warning must be issued.

Part of the reason I chose to write about dreams from a Christian perspective is to provide a counterbalance to the popular New Age movement. Several years ago, I felt that it had claimed dreams as its own, and I would like to reclaim this godly activity for followers of Jesus Christ. Hearing from God in dreams is a totally biblical activity—and Christians should never be afraid to embrace it.

Beware, however, of dream dictionaries written from a New Age perspective. When you read descriptions like "water symbolizes the deeper collective universal unconscious," or "the cross represents perfect balance, as in the Christ within, or Buddha consciousness," go ahead and close that book fast. Stop and investigate a little before buying, and especially read any biographical information, which may tell you the mindset of the author.

Thank you for reading this book. Sweetest dreams to you. But before you go, I have one more story for you—and it's a good one. Now please read the Epilogue.

EPILOGUE

When Dreams Come True

My younger daughter called me one day to tell me that her dad (my ex-husband) had unexpectedly called from a hospital. David had gone to the doctor for something he thought was routine, but when he was rushed on to the hospital, he figured it was pretty serious. That turned out to be the case. From the day of his diagnosis to the day of his death was only a brief forty days.

After he died I had many emotions to work through. But I had only *one* big question. Where was his soul? Had he ever accepted Christ? I had battled over the years, but who won the war? In the natural, there were mixed signals. He had returned to regular church attendance years before, but I knew that proved nothing for sure. Both of us had grown up in church without ever understanding the need for a personal Savior. Had he ever figured it out?

More than anything, I felt deeply sad. Now it was over. Nothing had turned out the way I expected when I said "yes" to God's invitation to live out the Vietnam dream. There had never been a hint of inclination to return to our marriage, no repentance that I knew of, and no apparent fruit of a changed life. Yet only God knows the heart, so I could still hope, figuring I'd have to wait till eternity to find out what had happened to my prayers.

Surprise! God graciously arranged a little eavesdropping episode for which I will be forever grateful. When word of David's illness got out, people began to call and drop by and some of them expressed concern about his spiritual condition. My daughter overheard one of the conversations. After a question about eternity was asked, David gave this strong, firm, sure reply, "I know who my Savior is; I know where I am going, and I'm not afraid to die."

When I heard this tremendously good news, it deeply pierced my soul. Oh my! He *was* won for eternity and I would see him again. I have lots of questions and plan to ask him the details of his story. I'd like to tell him my story, too, and also tell him about the dream, but perhaps he already knows that now. Proverbs 13:12 says, *"Hope deferred makes the heart sick, but desire fulfilled is a tree of life."* Yes! After hearing David's testimony at the end of his life, I can attest that it is true indeed.

Do you have dreams from God that still sit on a shelf after many years? Dusty, dry, and brittle, they defy your every attempt to understand or finalize them. Well, keep waiting. Don't give up. Ahead of you, I'm sure, is your own *"tree of life."* God bless you, and may your sleep be ever sweet.

ABOUT THE AUTHOR

Barbara Lardinais developed www.hannahscupboard. com in 2004 to provide Internet-based Christian teaching on prayer, Bible study, daily devotionals, and spiritual Q&A. She is an ordained minister through Apostolic Team Ministries, a graduate of Vision Christian Bible College, and was an associate pastor after a 26-year career in corporate America.

Author Contact Information

www.hannahscupboard.com

barbara@hannahscupboard.com

Made in the USA
Middletown, DE
03 October 2015